Walking the World in Wonder

A Children's Herbal

ELLEN EVERT HOPMAN

Photographs by Steven Foster

Healing Arts Press
Rochester, Vermont

To the Earth and Her creatures; to the furry, feathered, scaly, skinned, finned, slimy, and many-legged ones, and most especially to the green nations and to the little people and those who love them.

Healing Arts Press
One Park Street
Rochester, Vermont 05767
www.InnerTraditions.com

Healing Arts Press is a division of Inner Traditions International

Note to the reader: This book is intended as an informational guide. The remedies, approaches, and techniques described herein are meant to supplement, and not to be a substitute for, professional medical care or treatment. They should not be used to treat a serious ailment without prior consultation with a qualified health care professional. Children should use this book under the guidance and supervision of an adult.

LIBRARY OF CONGRESS CATALOGING-IN-PUBLICATION DATA

Hopman, Ellen Evert.
Walking the world in wonder : a children's herbal / Ellen Evert Hopman ;
photographs by Steven Foster.
p. cm.
ISBN 978-0-89281-878-5 (alk. paper)
1. Herbs—Therapeutic use—Juvenile literature. 2. Herbals—Juvenile literature.
[1. Herbs. 2. Plants, Useful.] I. Foster, Steven – ill. II. Title.
RM666.H33 H67 2000
615'.321—dc21   00-039575

Printed and bound in the United States by Versa Press, inc.

10   9   8   7   6   5   4   3

Text design and layout by Virginia L. Scott Bowman
This book was typeset in Stone Sans with Regular Joe as the display typeface

Watercolor illustrations by Jane MacKeil Alleman

Many thanks to Denise Gendreau and Kris Coutourier for their technical assistance. A special thanks to Lee Wood Juvan for her help and guidance. Thanks to the trees, flowers, and fairies of my garden for their unfailing inspiration.

CONTENTS

A Note to Parents
and Teachers   v

Introduction   1

The Wheel of the Year   5

Autumn

Barberry 11 • Burdock 13 • Fennel 15 •
Juniper 17 • Oak 19 • Partridgeberry 21 •
Walnut 23 • Wintergreen 25

Winter

Bayberry 29 • Holly 31 • Mistletoe 33 • Pine 35

Spring

Birch 39 • Chives 41 • Curled Dock 43 • Dandelion 45 • Ferns 47 •
Hawthorn Tree 49 • Hemlock Tree 51 • Horsetail 53 •
Lamb's-quarters 55 • Maple Tree 57 • Milkweed 59 • Plantain 61 •
Pokeweed 63 • Stinging Nettle 65 • Wild Strawberry 67 •
Trillium 69 • Violet 71 • Yarrow 73

Summer

Basil 77 • Bee Balm 79 • Blueberry 81 • Calendula 83 •
Wild Carrot 85 • Catnip 87 • Chamomile 89 • Cinquefoil 91 •
Club Moss 93 • Coltsfoot 95 • Comfrey 97 •
Daisy 99 • Daylily 101 • Dill 103 • Echinacea 105 •
Elderberry 107 • Ginger 109 • Goldenrod 111 •
Jerusalem Artichoke 113 • Lavender 115 • Lemon Balm 117 •
Marjoram 119 • Mint 121 • Nasturtium 123 • Parsley 125 •
Poplar 127 • Purslane 129 • Raspberry 131 •
Red Clover 133 • Rose 135 • Rosemary 137 • Sage 139 •
Staghorn Sumac 141 • Sunflower 143 • Thyme 145 •
Willow 147 • Witch Hazel 149

Epilogue   150
Bibliography   151
Resources   152

A NOTE TO PARENTS AND TEACHERS

This book is designed to encourage wonder. It can be used as a game whose object, like that of a scavenger hunt, is to find as many of the plants as possible, or it can be used as a field guide, a book to consult when you find yourself wandering through fields, woods, or gardens. Once upon a time, children would have learned about the many uses of plants—as food, as decoration, and most importantly, as medicine—from their elders. A wisewoman or man who had learned the ways of the plants would have guided children as they discovered the natural world around them. Our world is very different now, but plants still have much to teach us. This book will introduce children to the beauty and power of the herbs that still grow all around us—from rural fields or suburban yards to city parks and empty lots. The traditional medicinal uses for each plant are described along with suggestions for art projects, seasonal celebrations, and recipes.

Gathering Herbs with Your Child

Many of the projects in this book include making teas or edible treats from specific plants, tasks that will require guidance and supervision from an adult. If you and your child are new to the medicinal uses of herbs, you may want to enlist the assistance of a seasoned herbalist or gardener to help you identify plants. If you plan to use the herbs for edible or medicinal purposes, we suggest you purchase them from a reliable source, and reserve the herbs you gather for craft projects. Of course, you and your child should never ingest any herb if you are not sure that you have identified it correctly. As you gain experience with identifying herbs in the wild, you will be able to use what you gather yourself to treat minor ailments.

> ### Using Herbs Safely
> Some of the herbs mentioned in the book should not be ingested by children. Often there are safe medicinal uses for these herbs for adults, but they are not routinely recommended for children's use. Entries that contain this symbol ☹ indicate plants that should not be eaten!
> The safety issues of herb use during pregnancy are beyond the scope of this book, which is geared toward children. Pregnant and lactating women should not use *any* of the herbs mentioned in this book without consulting an herbalist or an herbal especially designed for their unique needs.

Using Homemade Medicines

Most children are excited when they learn that the plants they see in their backyard or on their walk to school can help them feel better when they have a sore throat or bruised knee. Even fussy kids will be thrilled to take their "homemade medicine" with the addition of a little honey. But children should be taught that with the exception of very mild herbs (such as peppermint or chamomile, for example), many herbal teas are indeed medicines and not for daily use. Medicinal teas or preparations should be used occasionally rather than routinely; even safe herbs, like most substances, can cause side effects if taken frequently or in excess. Any serious ailments should always be brought to the attention of a health care professional. Unless an entry states otherwise, a child's dosage for a medicinal herbal tea is 1 cup per day, taken in $1/4$ cup doses (or sips, if indicated) between meals; adults can have up to 2 cups per day.

Hints for Small Hunters and Gatherers

Attention to a few key details will make your gathering experience safer and more satisfying. Because lead and emissions from cars tend to be concentrated in the soil near the roadsides, be sure that any plants you plan to consume are gathered at least 1,000 feet from any busy road or highway. Likewise, city lots and suburban lawns may have been sprayed with pesticides or fertilizers that can contaminate the plants growing there. Be sure that you do not consume any plants unless you are certain that they are free of chemicals. Any wild greens you gather should be soaked for 20 minutes in a gallon of cold water to which you have added 2 tablespoon of vinegar or salt. The soaking will remove any parasites or "wild things" clinging to the greens! Then they should be carefully washed and rinsed as usual.

Herbal identification was an integral part of children's everyday education until very recent times. In this age of synthetic medicines that are often expensive and sometimes have harsh effects on the body, it is important that this knowledge be preserved and handed down to future generations. Powerful and nourishing healing agents are all around us in the garden, field, and forest. My hope is that this small volume will pass some traditional herbal wisdom on to children and inspire a lifetime of inquiry into the magic and beauty of the green world.

INTRODUCTION

Long before people bought medicine or food at a store, they learned to use the wild plants growing all around them. They watched animals to see which plants were good to eat and which plants were poisonous. They experimented and learned which plants could heal people when they were hurt or sick. People passed their knowledge on to their children and grandchildren for generations. This book will help you learn the names of many different kinds of plants and show you how they can be used for medicine, food, and fun.

Using this Book

On the next page is a checklist of some plants that you can find in the fields and forests of the northern temperate zone. The entries in this book will tell you the plant's common name—the name in English that you will find in the checklist—along with its Latin name in parenthesis. Scientists always use Latin plant names to avoid confusion. Different countries, and sometimes different areas of the same country, use different common names for the same plant, but a plant's Latin name is the same all over the world. There is also a photograph beside each entry to help you identify the plants you find. Many of these herbs have healing properties, but not all parts of all plants are good to eat, so be sure you use them only with the help of an adult. Have fun finding as many as you can!

Some plants are not good for children to eat at all. Do not eat the plant when you see this symbol ☹. Never eat any plant that you find on your own without asking an adult's permission!

Making Your Own Herbal

You can make your own herbal "catalogue" of plants that you have collected and pressed. To do this, you will need an old phone book, some watercolor paper, and some clear, self-sticking shelf paper, which you can find in most craft or hardware stores. Gather your plants on a dry day, after the morning dew has evaporated. It is important that the plants be dry when you pick them. Carefully press the leaves and flowers in the old phone book. Phone books work well because the pages are so absorbent. Take your phone book with you on your field trips—you never know when you might find a plant you have been searching for! When you get home, put your phone book on a table or countertop and place a heavy book on top of it (a dictionary is good). Let your plants sit like this for a week.

The plants are ready to mount when they still have their green color but are completely dry. This is important—if there is any moisture left in the plant, mold will form under the plastic. Take your pressed plant and place it on a sheet of watercolor paper. You might want to write the plant's name on the bottom of the paper to help you remember it. Then cover the whole sheet of paper with a layer of clear, self-sticking shelf paper. Trim the edges of the shelf paper so that they are even with the edges of the watercolor paper. Plants preserved like this will keep their color for years.

Helping Our Plant Friends

A note about "green etiquette": whenever you gather plants you must be sure that there are at least seven individuals left so that the species can continue to reproduce. This ensures that enough plants will remain to form seeds, which will grow into new plants for animals and people to use and enjoy. Never take more plants than you will use, even if there are plenty. It is also nice to leave a gift when you take something from Nature. Native Americans traditionally leave tobacco, sage, or cornmeal. The ancient European custom was to give a gift of honey, vervain (an herb), or apple cider. You can leave a coin, a pinch of cornmeal, some honey, cider, fertilizer, or a small shell; but you might choose to sing a song or say a prayer instead.

Some plants are in danger of becoming extinct. This means that if people do not begin to protect them, there will be no more left anywhere in the world.

2

If a plant is at risk, the entry will tell you so. These plants are special and should never be picked from the wild. If you grow them in your garden, then it's OK to pick them.

Please remember to give thanks to our green sisters and brothers. Without plants we would have no food to eat, no medicine, no furniture or homes, no clothing, no air to breathe. We depend on them for our very lives and they need our help too!

Put a check mark in the box next to each plant you have found.

AUTUMN

- ☐ Barberry
- ☐ Burdock
- ☐ Fennel
- ☐ Juniper
- ☐ Oak
- ☐ Partridgeberry
- ☐ Walnut
- ☐ Wintergreen

WINTER

- ☐ Bayberry
- ☐ Holly ☹
- ☐ Mistletoe ☹
- ☐ Pine

SPRING

- ☐ Birch
- ☐ Chives
- ☐ Curled Dock
- ☐ Dandelion
- ☐ Ferns

SPRING (continued)

- ☐ Hawthorn
- ☐ Hemlock Tree
- ☐ Horsetail ☹
- ☐ Lamb's-quarters
- ☐ Maple Tree
- ☐ Milkweed
- ☐ Plantain
- ☐ Pokeweed ☹
- ☐ Stinging Nettle
- ☐ Wild Strawberry
- ☐ Trillium
- ☐ Violet
- ☐ Yarrow

SUMMER

- ☐ Basil
- ☐ Bee Balm
- ☐ Blueberry
- ☐ Calendula
- ☐ Wild Carrot
- ☐ Catnip

SUMMER (continued)

☐ Chamomile

☐ Cinquefoil

☐ Club Moss ☹

☐ Coltsfoot

☐ Comfrey

☐ Daisy

☐ Daylily

☐ Dill

☐ Echinacea

☐ Elderberry

☐ Ginger

☐ Goldenrod

☐ Jerusalem Artichoke

☐ Lavender

☐ Lemon Balm

☐ Marjoram

☐ Mint

☐ Nasturtium

☐ Parsley

☐ Poplar

☐ Purslane

☐ Raspberry

☐ Red Clover

☐ Rose

☐ Rosemary

☐ Sage

☐ Staghorn Sumac

☐ Sunflower

☐ Thyme

☐ Willow ☹

☐ Witch Hazel

THE WHEEL
OF THE YEAR

In ancient times, before people had electric lights and television sets and grocery stores, they paid more attention to the natural world than we do today. They noticed sunrise and sunset, the phases of the moon, new leaves on trees, the birth of baby animals, the ripening of berries, the first frost and the first snowfall. Their very survival depended on understanding and working with the rhythms of nature.

If they didn't pay attention to the ways of the plants and animals around them, they wouldn't have enough to eat. When they worked carefully with nature, they were able to feast in times of plenty and to survive the long, cold winters as well. It makes sense that their festivals and celebrations marked the changing of the seasons, thanking nature for the gifts of each.

Even though we buy most of our food today in the supermarket, turn up the thermostat when we feel cold, and turn on the lights when it gets dark outside, in the end we're still dependent on nature and it's still important for us to notice, honor, and give thanks for the ways of the Earth. Learning about wild plants is one way to do that. Another fun way is to celebrate the seasonal festivals of our ancestors—the ancient circle or wheel of the year.

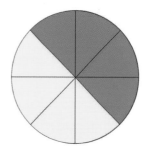

Every day has two halves, a dark half when you go to sleep, called *night* and a light half when you wake up, called *day*. The year also has a dark half and a light half. These times of darkness and light are determined by how much sunlight we see. The dark half begins with the fall equinox, a day when night and day are of equal length. After this point there will be more hours of darkness in each day. The light half begins with the spring equinox, a day when night and day are once again of equal length. Each day after this will have more hours of light. In between these two special days are many festivals and holidays that mark the changes of the sacred Earth year.

Halloween, or Samhain (Celtic; pronounced "sow-in"), is the festival marking the beginning of the dark half of the year, the time before the light and fire of nature is born. We celebrate this holiday on the last night of October by dressing up as ghosts and goblins because this is the festival of the dead—those who no longer have a human body. At this time, plants are in the form of seeds waiting to be born.

The next festival is the winter solstice or Yule. This festival occurs on the longest night of the year (usually December 21). From this day and night forward, the light of the Sun gradually increases. We celebrate by putting lights on evergreen trees such as firs and pines, which are symbols of immortality because they do not lose their leaves in winter.

We hang round wreaths, symbolic of the returning Sun, on our doors. We also decorate the house with evergreens as a sign to the nature spirits that they will find a warm welcome in our home during the cold and dark season. At this time we give thanks to the dark for giving us rest.

On February 2 we celebrate Imbolc (Celtic; pronounced "ihm-bolg"). Imbolc falls in the middle of the dark half of the year. This is the time when female farm animals such as ewes (female sheep) give birth and start to produce milk. This is also the festival of Brighid—the Celtic Goddess of fire, smithcraft, poetry, and healing. Some people today celebrate the day as Groundhog Day, a day when the groundhog, or woodchuck, appears from his burrow. If the groundhog sees its shadow, traditionally it means winter weather will return. In Europe it is the hedgehog or badger that emerges to view its shadow. Originally it was a snake who emerged from the Earth to see her shadow.

The snake has always been an animal sacred to Goddesses because the Earth is seen as female in many cultures. The snake goes deep into the Earth to learn Her secrets of wisdom and healing. In this season, the fires of life begin to stir in seeds that are deep underground.

The next festival is the spring equinox (usually March 21). Here the days and nights are of equal length. In ancient times there was a Teutonic (Germanic) Goddess called Eostre (Germanic; pronounced "ee-o-stra"). Her sacred symbols were the hare and the egg. People would paint their dreams and wishes on eggs and bury them in the ground. This was so that Mother Earth could use the life force in these "animal seeds" and make the wishes painted on them come true. Today, we call the festival "Easter" and we still use rabbits and eggs as symbols for the celebration. This is the season when bulbs and blossoms first appear.

May Day, or Beltane (Celtic; pronounced "bell-tain"), is often celebrated on May 1, but in the past it was not official until the hawthorn tree blossomed. Beltane marks the beginning of the light half of the year. By now the light is very strong and many flowers have started to open. We celebrate by dancing around the maypole and by giving baskets of flowers to family and friends. The maypole symbolizes the strengthening Sun which penetrates the Earth and helps Her to nourish the plants. Dancing around the maypole helps to "wake up" the Earth so She can do Her work.

The light is strongest at midsummer (usually June 21). This is the longest day of the year. We celebrate by being out in the Sun and even by camping out all night because the night is so short. We build bonfires in celebration of the Sun's bright light and we give thanks for all the blessings He brings; warmth, light, and the green plants and trees. This is the last day to pick tree leaves for medicine. After this they contain too much natural insecticide.

The first harvest festival occurs on August 1, halfway through the light half of the year. Lammas or Lughnasad (Celtic; pronounced "loo-nas-ad") was once called the "Loaf Mass" by people who went to church because at this time the first fruits of the harvest, especially the new grain, were brought to the church to be blessed. Today many people still pray at this time of year that the rest of the harvest will be bountiful.

Next we come to the fall equinox, when night and day are again of equal length. The light and warmth of summer begin to fade and the peaceful darkness of winter approaches. We celebrate by feasting on the abundant produce of our gardens and fields. And we end the year by storing our herbs and vegetables for the coming dark season.

Finally we return to Samhain and the wheel of the year is complete.

Autumn

The goldenrod is yellow;
The corn is turning brown;
The trees in apple orchards
With fruit are bending down.
The gentian's bluest fringes
Are curling in the sun;
In dusty pods the milkweed
Its hidden silk has spun.
The sedges flaunt their harvest
In every meadow nook;
And asters by the brookside
Make asters in the brook.
From dewy lanes at morning
The grapes' sweet odors rise;
At noon the roads all flutter
With yellow butterflies.
By all these lovely tokens
September days are here,
With summer's best of weather
And autumn's best of cheer.

Helen Hunt Jackson,
"September"

BARBERRY
(*Berberis vulgaris*)

I am the barberry. I am found in open fields and sometimes in people's yards. I am a yellow-flowering shrub. Look for my flowers from spring to early summer. My berries change colors and they are oblong. I have golden berries in spring, green berries in summer, and red berries in fall. My berries are edible but only when they are red and fully ripe in the late summer or early autumn. I also have little thorns at the base of my leaves. Look for me on people's lawns and in fields. Can you find me?

You can rub ripe barberries on your gums when you have a mouth sore.

BURDOCK
(Arctium lappa)

I am burdock. I have little burrs that stick to your pants and all over dogs in the fall. I am a biennial plant (I have a two-year life cycle). The best time to use my roots is in the fall of my first year when I have large crinkly leaves that are green and hairy on top and downy gray underneath. By my second year I have purple flowers from summer to early fall and seeds form inside my burrs, but my root is not as good.

Many people boil my root and eat it as a vegetable. In Japan you'd find me for sale in grocery stores! In Japanese I am called "gobo."

Can you find me?

A tea made from burdock root, fresh or dried, is a good blood cleanser and liver tonic. Simmer 1 teaspoon of root per cup of water for 20 minutes and take up to 1 cup per day.

You can also use a wash of my leaves for skin sores, pimples, and poison ivy. Have an adult help you chop a handful of fresh leaves and put them in a pan. Add enough cold water to cover the leaves and simmer briefly. Turn off the heat and let the leaves steep for 20 minutes. Let the liquid cool and then strain out the leaves. Using cotton balls or an old washcloth, apply the wash to the affected skin. *Do not drink the wash made from the leaves; use it only on your skin.*

FENNEL
(*Foeniculum vulgare*)

I am fennel. I belong to the *Umbelliferae* family (plants that look like inside-out umbrellas). I am related to the carrot, and my root is long and carrot-shaped, but it is not orange. My leaves are lacy and delicate like those of the carrot. My flowers are yellow and appear from summer to fall. You can gather my seeds in the fall to make a tea for coughs and upset stomachs.

Can you find me? I am probably growing in someone's herb garden.

To make a tea, pour 1 cup of boiling water over 1 teaspoon of crushed fennel seeds (you can crush the seeds with the back of a spoon), and let the seeds soak for 20 minutes. If you have aniseed or caraway seed, you can add these to the mix. Use equal parts to total 1 teaspoon of seed per cup of water.

JUNIPER
(Juniperus communis)

I am juniper. I have berries that are green one year and dark blue the next. I am an evergreen and you will find me in open fields. My berries are good for the stomach and help digestion. Gather a few to chew on when they are fully ripe or make them into a tea. To make a tea, steep 2 teaspoons of juniper berries in a cup of freshly boiled water for 10 minutes. A child can have $\frac{1}{2}$ cup per day for up to one week. (Avoid large doses and long-term use. Those with kidney problems should not use juniper.)

You can also use me to make a smudge stick. Find an adult friend to help you do this. You will need juniper, cedar, and some sage—which you can find fresh in the garden or in the grocery store. Cut 12-inch sections off of a juniper shrub (use only the ends of the branches). You can cut the ends of cedar branches too. Get an old newspaper and lay the herbs on top of it. Place the juniper, cedar, and sage on top of each other so that all of the stems are pointing the same way. Roll the paper tightly around the herbs to make a cigar-shaped bundle about a foot long. Tie the bundle with string at both ends and in the middle to hold it together. Place the bundle in a warm (100°F) oven for an hour. Open the bundle to see if it is completely dry and holds together like a "stick." If it does not, tie it closed again and put it in the oven for another 30 to 60 minutes.

Throw away the newspaper and burn the smudge stick like incense to scent a room or an outdoor area. Always ask an adult for help when burning a smudge stick.

In Native American tradition, a smudge stick is burned to prepare an area for prayer. The scent cleanses the air and brings peace. It also keeps away flying bugs. Native Americans use white sage and cedar in their smudge sticks. White sage grows in the western United States. In the east, we use kitchen sage or common sage, which work equally well.

OAK
(*Quercus spp.*)

I am the oak tree. My roots grow as deep as my branches are high. I bear nuts with little hats. You can carry one of my acorns to bring good luck. In olden times Druids worshipped beneath my branches. Druids were the priests and priestesses of the ancient Celts. They would plant oaks in groves—circles of trees—and do rituals there. Oak groves are still enjoyed for outdoor celebrations today.

A wash made from oak bark will help heal skin problems such as wet, weepy eczema, rashes, and sores. To make a skin treatment, please use only bark from a twig or bark gathered from a fallen tree. (If you *girdle,* or cut, a ring of bark from the trunk of a living tree, you will kill it.) When gathering tree bark for medicine, you will need to get the *cambrium,* the thin layer of tissue underneath the tough outer bark. The outer bark is not strong enough for medicine. Simmer 1 tablespoon of oak bark in 1 pint of water for 10 minutes. Soak a clean cotton cloth in the warm oak wash and wrap it around the affected part. This is called a "fomentation."

You can also use oak leaves to make a compress for insect bites and minor scratches. For a compress, soak a handful of leaves in freshly boiled water until they are soft. Then apply them to the affected area (be sure they are not too hot!). Wrap a cloth soaked in oak wash around the area to hold the leaves in place. Leave the compress on for 10 to 30 minutes.

PARTRIDGEBERRY
(*Mitchella repens*)

I grow where the woods are deep and moist. My stems trail along the forest floor under my leaves. My white flowers are funnel-shaped and appear in pairs from spring to summer. In autumn and winter you can find me easily because I have bright red berries and small, dark green leaves. Native Americans used my medicine to help women through childbirth. I also help people fall asleep. I have many other names: checkerberry, beeberry, deerberry, twinberry, box-berry, chickenberry, cowberry, pigeon-berry, snakeberry, and teaberry—to name just a few. I am an endangered species because I particularly like to grow near trees and tree stumps in mature forests. Old forests are getting harder and harder to find! Can you find me? Hint: My leaves *do not* have a distinctive smell. Crush a leaf and see if it smells like wintergreen, which also has red berries.

Because there are so few of me left in the forest, please do not pick me. If you want to include me in your scrapbook of plants, please draw a picture or take a photograph of me. If you close your eyes at night and concentrate on me, I will send you a dream of my shady forest home to help you fall asleep more quickly!

WALNUT
(Juglans nigra; J. regia)

I am the walnut tree. A native North American tree, I can grow up to 75 feet tall. I have a smooth gray bark and a compound leaf (a leaf made up of many smaller leaves sharing a common stem). In autumn you can gather my nuts when they are covered by a green hull. You have probably tasted my crunchy nuts in chocolate chip cookies or brownies. Can you find me?

The hull is the soft green covering around the hard brown nut. Gather my nuts when the hulls are still green if you want to use the nuts for medicine. If you peel the hull off—ask an adult for help because it will require a sharp knife—you can use the hulls to make a healing salve for minor skin irritations (see Plantain, page 61).

Walnut hulls can also be used to dye wool a rich, dark brown. You'll need the help of an adult for this activity. First, you will need a loose skein of real wool yarn (acrylic will not work!). If your yarn is in a ball, make a skein by wrapping a strand of yarn around and around the back of a chair. Tie the skein loosely in several places with cotton string to keep it from getting tangled in the dye bath. Gather about 50 to 75 walnut hulls and soak them overnight in a big pot of water (a stainless or enamel soup pot works best). Put the pot on a stove and simmer the hulls for an hour. Soak the skein of wool in warm water while the hulls simmer. Strain the hulls from the dye bath. Add the wet yarn and simmer for an hour. Turn off the heat and let the dye bath cool. Once the bath has cooled, you can remove the yarn, rinse it in clear water, and hang it to dry. Your beautiful hand-dyed yarn is ready to use!

Hint: Wear rubber gloves and an old apron when you peel walnuts or your hands and clothes will turn brown. I am proud of my walnut oil, which is so rich it is used to make a furniture stain!

WINTERGREEN
(Gaultheria procumbens)

I am wintergreen. You can find me in the deep woods. I have opposite, toothed leaves and shiny red berries in autumn and winter. My nodding white flowers bloom from spring to early fall. If you think you've found me, pinch a leaf off to see if it smells minty before you pick some more. You can eat my berries or add them to salads. An easy way to enjoy me is to chew my leaves like chewing gum. You can also make a tea of my leaves for a sore throat, a sore in the mouth, an upset stomach, or a headache. You can also soak a cloth in the tea to make a fomentation for skin problems and inflammation (see page 19 for fomentation directions).

To make wintergreen tea, you should collect its leaves in the spring. Steep 1 teaspoon of fresh or dried leaf in a cup of freshly boiled water for 5 minutes. Drink 1 cup 1 teaspoonful at a time throughout the day.

Winter

I stood beside a hill
   Smooth with new-laid snow,
A single star looked out
   From the cold evening glow.
There was no other creature
   That saw what I could see—
I stood and watched the evening star
   As long as it watched me.

**Sara Teasdale,
"February Twilight"**

BAYBERRY
(Myrica cerifera)

I am the bayberry. My leaves are wider at the tips and my yellowish flowers grow in clusters below my leaves. I bloom from spring to summer. You will find me growing near the ocean. I am an evergreen—I stay green all year. In the winter I have small, round fruits covered with a grayish white wax. Use my wax in candles or soap and my leaves and berries in Yuletide decorations. It takes one bushel of my berries to make 4 pounds of wax, so be sure to collect them only where I grow in profusion.

To collect bayberry wax, place berries in a old pot and cover with water. Bring to a boil. Lower the heat and let simmer long enough for the wax to release from the berries. Remove from heat, skim the wax off the water with a perforated spoon, and drop onto wax paper or foil. Allow the wax to cool before touching it. (You can let the water and berries cool and then add them to your compost pile.)

The wax is a fragrant addition to homemade soaps or candles. Place a little bayberry wax in your soap or candle molds before you pour in the hot liquid.

HOLLY ☹
(Ilex acquifolium; I. opaca)

I am the holly. Although I am often trimmed so I will fit in people's gardens, I am actually a tree and can grow up to 90 feet tall. You will recognize me in winter by my spiny, waxy leaves and my bright red berries. *My berries are not for eating; they would make you very sick!* I have small, white flowers in May and June. I am an evergreen and keep my leaves all winter long. I symbolize eternal life and remind everyone that life goes on—even when all the other trees are bare and plants are sleeping under the snow. In ancient times I was a tree sacred to warriors because my sharp, thorny needles are tough and enduring and my vibrant red berries are the color of blood.

People like to put me on their doors or use me for indoor decorations in the dark wintertime. They often make me into a wreath. The wreath is a circle that symbolizes the Sun. Winter solstice is a solar festival because we are celebrating the Sun's return. Have you seen me?

MISTLETOE ☹
(*Viscum album*)

I am mistletoe. Have you seen me in holiday decorations? I have yellowish green opposite leaves and pale yellow or green flowers that grown into sticky white berries. *My berries are poisonous so never eat them!* I am a very mysterious plant. I am a parasite that burrows into the bark of a tree and lives off of the tree's sap. Most plants are heliotropic, which means that they stretch and bend themselves toward the sunlight. I don't do that at all. Instead, I grow in every direction and hang in bunches off the branches of trees. I was a sacred herb of the ancient Druids who wore white when they came to pick me six days after the new moon.

An old Scandinavian custom from Viking times is to hang mistletoe over the doorway at Yuletide as a symbol of love. This tradition is rooted in myths passed down for generations: Baldur, the Shining God in Scandinavian mythology, had a terrible dream that he was going to die. Frigg, the Mother of All Gods, asked every living thing to promise not to harm Baldur in any way. But she forgot to ask Mistletoe. One day the gods were playing a game of throwing things at Baldur because he could not be hurt. Loki, the trickster who was fond of mischief, decided to sabotage Frigg. Loki gave Mistletoe to the blind god Hodur so he would have something to throw at Baldur during the game. When Hodur threw Mistletoe at Baldur, he fell down dead. Everyone went into mourning because they missed Baldur and they begged for him to be brought back to life. Eventually he was and the light of his spirit shone on the Earth once more. Mistletoe was put under the care of the Goddess of Love, who enjoined everyone to kiss under its branches. That is why we kiss under the mistletoe at Yule, bringing the warmth of love into the darkest part of the year!

PINE
(*Pinus spp.*)

I am the pine. My leaves are called "needles" and they grow in clusters of five. My seeds grow in pine cones. If you look closely, you will see that my pine cones grow in a sun-wise (clockwise) spiral. I keep my green color all winter, which is why I am an *evergreen.* You bring me into your house at Yule to remind the world that life never dies. Have you seen me?

White pine (*Pinus strobus*) is the best pine tree for tea. It is slightly antiseptic and high in vitamins C and A. Its inner bark, the knots found in its soft wood, and young white pine needles can all be simmered to make a tea that helps coughs and colds. White pine tea can also be added to the bathtub for a relaxing soak that soothes aching muscles, tense nerves, and helps clear the lungs. Use the twigs, young shoots, and needles, and break them into 1-inch pieces. To brew pine tea, take 1 teaspoon of pine and simmer in 1 cup of water for 20 minutes. A child can take $1/2$ cup sipped throughout the day. An adult can have 1 cup.

Spring

'Tis merry in green wood—thus runs the old lay—
In the gladsome month of lively May,
When the wild birds' song on stem and spray
   Invites to forest bower;
Then rears the ash his airy crest,
Then shines the birch in silver vest,
And the beech in glistening leaves is drest,
And dark between shows the oak's proud breast,
   Like a chieftain's frowning tower;
Though a thousand branches join their screen,
Yet the broken sunbeams glance between,
And tip the leaves with lighter green,
   With brighter tints the flowers;
Dull is the heart that loves not then
The deep recess of the wildwood glen
Where roe and red-deer find sheltering den,
   When the Sun is in his power.

**Walter Scott,
"'Tis Merry in the Greenwood"**

BIRCH
(*Betula alba; B. lenta*)

I am the birch tree. My trunk can be white, black, or gray. When bark uncurls from a white birch tree, you can write on it just like on a scroll of paper (but please don't pull my new pink bark off!). You can recognize black birch by crushing a leaf or twig and sniffing—black birch smells like wintergreen. My leaves are bright green and lighter underneath. They have serrated edges like the teeth on a saw and are slightly hairy. My flowers are called "catkins," and they droop gracefully from my branches in the spring. Native Americans once used white birch bark to make canoes, so some people call it "canoe birch." Boil my young leaves and twigs and leaves in water to help heal skin problems or add the tea to your bath. Can you find me?

To make an external wash from white birch, use 1 tablespoon of fresh leaves for each cup of water; simmer for 5 minutes and then steep for 2 hours. Soak a cloth in the wash to make a fomentation to treat skin problems or add the tea to bath water (see page 19 for fomentation directions).

To make ginger ale, you can make a strong batch of black birch twig and ginger-root tea, and dissolve honey into it while it is still warm. Store this mixture in your refrigerator, keeping it tightly closed, for several months. When you want ginger ale, just fill a glass about $1/3$ full with the black birch twig tea and fill the rest with a cold sparkling water or seltzer water.

CHIVES
(Allium schoenoprasum)

We are chives. You can find us growing in people's herb gardens. We are perennials—when you plant us in the garden, we come back year after year. We have fuzzy pink flowers that you can gather and hang upside down in bunches to dry. You can eat out flowers! Sprinkle them on salads or soups. Pick our green spears before they flower, chop them, and add them to salads and soups. You can also sprinkle them on hot baked potatoes. We grow well with carrots and we can be frozen for later use.

   Hint: If you grow chives in your garden, cut them back once or twice in the summer to keep them fresh and green with new growth. Chives can be frozen and used in the winter. Simply put the cut chives in a zip-top baggie and freeze them.

CURLED DOCK
(*Rumex crispus*)

I am curled dock. I have crinkly leaves. I also have a long yellow taproot so some people call me yellow dock. My stem grows 1 to 3 feet high, and my leaves are pointed with a wavy edge. At high summer I bloom with pale green flowers. Later in the season I bear hard, heart-shaped seeds. You can put my root in salves to heal the skin (see Plantain, page 61, for salve directions) or boil my roots to make an iron-rich, laxative tea. Boil 1 teaspoon of chopped fresh or dried root per cup of water and simmer for 20 minutes. Take $1/2$ cup to 1 cup a day. Take less to treat diarrhea; more will have a laxative effect.

You can collect curled dock leaves early in the spring when they are no more than 4 inches high. Wash the leaves in cool water. Place them in a pan with enough cool water to cover them. Allow them to boil for 5 minutes, pour off the water, add fresh water, and boil for 5 more minutes. Drain and serve with butter, a pinch of salt, and a squeeze of lemon.

Hint: When you dig up a root or when you pick any wild plant, soak it in enough water to cover with a few tablespoons of salt or vinegar for about 20 minutes. This will make any parasites fall off, and it will also be easier to scrub off the dirt.

DANDELION
(Taraxacum officinale)

I am the dandelion. I have bright yellow flowers that look like little suns. I grow in the grass and I really like people. You can eat my leaves—or "greens" as they are called—very early in the spring before I flower. You can make a tea from my roots that is good for your liver and joints. I also help with constipation, fever, and upset stomachs. Some people make wine from my flowers. Can you find me?

A dandelion salad is slightly bitter but very good for you. Pick my leaves in the early spring before they flower. Soak them for 15 minutes in cool water to which you've added a pinch of salt. Rinse them and spin dry with a salad spinner or pat dry with a paper towel. Dress with olive oil, lemon juice, and sea salt. Try adding violet blossoms, chives, and grated carrot for a wild salad.

To make a *Dandelion Tonic,* use a pot with a good lid and steep 2 teaspoons of chopped, fresh, dandelion greens in 1 cup of freshly boiled water for about 20 minutes. A child can have up to $1/2$ cup per day; an adult 1 cup. To make a tonic of the roots, dandelion roots can be dug in early spring or fall. Simmer 2 teaspoons of the chopped root in 1 cup of water for 20 minutes in a covered saucepan. A child can take 2 tablespoons 3 times a day; the adult dosage is 3 tablespoons 6 times a day.

You can also juice my leaves in a juicer in the spring and take 1 teaspoon in milk three times a day. They are full of vitamins A and C. Some people may experience skin irritation from the latex in dandelion stems and leaves, so wash your hands thoroughly after picking them.

To enjoy a bit of garden magic, when you find a "puff ball" made up of dandelion seeds think about a wish as you blow on it gently. Or let the wind carry the seeds away. The seeds will carry your wish out to the world and help it come true.

FERNS
(*Pteridium aquilinum; Pteretis pensylvanica*)

We are ferns. We grow on the forest floor. Can you find us? Our young shoots or baby ferns are known as "fiddleheads" because in the early spring they look like the neck of a violin. Fiddleheads are good to eat in the spring.

Bracken ferns are common ferns found in fields and forests. In the spring we have three little claws that make us look like an eagle's talons. Later in the summer we grow into dark green, three-forked plants.

Ostrich ferns have beautiful emerald green fiddleheads that are covered with thin brown scales. We grow in moist woods and near streams. By summer our fronds will develop into huge plumes like giant bird feathers, and we will have dark brown fronds in the center of our plumes. You can wipe off the fuzz and scales and eat us like asparagus. Gather us in the early part of the year when we are still tightly coiled.

Gather bracken ferns early in the spring when they are 6 to 8 inches tall and their "eagle's talons" are still unfurled. Rub off the wooly hairs. Ostrich ferns should be picked when they are 6 inches tall and still curled. Rinse thoroughly in cool water. In a saucepan, add the fiddleheads with enough water to cover and bring to a boil. Add more water and simmer for another 10 to 15 minutes. Drain and eat with butter and a squeeze of lemon or toss in a salad.

47

HAWTHORN TREE
(Crataegus spp.)

I am known as the "May tree" because in olden times people celebrated May Day on the day when my blossoms first opened. I have toothy leaves and thorns. My flowers are usually white with 5 petals. In the fall I have red berries with 1 to 5 seeds. There are almost 1,000 species of hawthorns in the United States, and I am most common in the eastern and central states. I also grow in Europe and China. I am a favorite tree of the fairies. A solitary hawthorn on a hill or next to a well often marks the entrance to the fairy realm. Can you find me?

You can use hawthorn flowers and berries to help you sleep and to strengthen your heart. To make a calming tea, use 1 teaspoon of hawthorn flowers in 1 cup of freshly boiled water and steep for 15 minutes. A child can have ½ cup twice a day; an adult 1 cup twice a day (for occasional use; one week on, one week off).

HEMLOCK TREE
(*Tsuga canadensis*)

I am the hemlock. I can grow from 50 to 100 feet tall in moist woods. I have short green needles and brownish gray bark with rough scales. My seed cones are tiny—less than 1 inch long. In the spring when my leaf tips are pale green you can eat them. They taste a little bit sour like a lemon—that tells you they contain vitamin C. Native Americans learned to eat hemlock by watching the deer. Each time you see a hemlock, remember to thank the deer for passing on their wisdom.

You can make a tea of the hemlock tree's young twigs and needles for skin sores, for use as a sore throat gargle, or as a mouthwash for mouth sores. The best time to gather hemlock is in the spring when the tips of the branches are pale green with new growth. As the summer approaches, the tips will darken and will not taste as good. (For external use as a wash it does not matter when you gather the twig tips.) To make a tea, simmer 1 teaspoon of the pale green tips of new twigs per cup of water for 10 minutes.

HORSETAIL ☹
(Equisetum arvense)

I am horsetail. I have a stiff stem with many joints and no leaves. I live near water in moist, sandy soil and grow from 4 to 7 inches tall. The pioneers called me "scouring rush" because they used my bunched-up stems to scour pots and pans. I am a very ancient plant. Three hundred million years ago my relatives were 30 feet tall. The forests they formed eventually turned into the coal deposits we have on Earth today. I am so ancient that I don't even have leaves (leaves and flowers came much later in plant evolution).

A wash made from horsetail is good for minor cuts and skin irritations. To make, steep 4 teaspoons of the dried plant in 1 cup of freshly boiled water for 1 hour. Gently wash or briefly soak the affected area.

Horsetail contains silica, which makes it abrasive. To make scouring pad for pots and pans, collect a small bunch of horsetail stems and let them dry in the sun until they can be snapped in pieces. Tie several pieces in a small bundle with string, and keep the bundles handy in the kitchen.

LAMB'S-QUARTERS
(Chenopodium album)

I am lamb's-quarters. I stand straight up! My stems are covered with a faint dusting of white powder and are streaked with red or light green lines. My oval leaves have gently wavey edges and a whitish, mealy covering that makes me look gray. I bloom from the summer to the fall with tiny green or red flowers. I am also called "wild spinach" because you can eat me just like spinach. I grow in areas where the soil has been disturbed such as gardens, yards, meadows, fields, ditches, and roadsides. Look for me especially in areas where sheep used to live!

Collect my leaves in the spring and early summer. Gather a lot because they will shrink when you cook them. Lightly steam or sauté just like spinach and serve with a little butter and salt.

MAPLE TREE
(Acer saccharinum)

I am the maple. I grow in woods and fields and reach 60 to 130 feet in height. My leaves are probably familiar to you—they have five points called *lobes*. A maple leaf appears on the Canadian flag. When my leaves are very small you can eat them in salads. People tap my trunk to get my sap. When my sap is boiled, it becomes maple syrup. Have you had my sap on your pancakes?

Maple syrup makes a very good sugar substitute. Because it is not a refined sugar, like white sugar, it will not rot your teeth as much. Maple syrup also has the advantage of having trace minerals like iron and calcium.

For a tasty summer drink, try making maple syrup lemonade. Simply mix 2 tablespoons of maple syrup and 2 tablespoons of lemon juice and add ice and water to taste.

MILKWEED
(Asclepias syriaca)

I am milkweed. I grow in open fields. My leaves are downy and grayish green, and my flowers are dusty purple or white and grow in clusters. My seed pods are pointy with little warts on the outside. I am a favorite plant of the monarch butterfly. Look for caterpillars and cocoons on my leaves as the summer progresses. In the late spring you can gather my green, unopened buds and steam, sauté, or boil them and serve them with butter. (Taste a bit before you eat a whole serving; some people find them disagreeable.) In the fall my pods are filled with soft, downy floss. You can gather my floss and use it to stuff toys and pillows, or make a wish and blow it to the wind!

Milkweed has a white milky sap that is *not good to eat* but helps warts go away. Break off a twig or pull off a leaf and squeeze the sap directly on the wart. Allow it to dry. Repeat daily until the wart disappears. (Do not apply to broken skin and do not get the sap in your eyes, nose, or mouth.)

Milkweed floss is waterproof and was once used to fill life preservers. If you sew a tiny pillow and stuff it *tightly* with milkweed floss, it should float!

PLANTAIN
(*Plantago spp.*)

We are the plantains. There are many kinds of plantains. Some have long, thin, ribbed leaves *(P. lanceolata),* and some have fat, round, ribbed leaves *(P. major).* Our flower stalks grow from 6 to 30 inches tall and are tipped by spikes of tiny white flowers that bloom from spring to fall. We grow on lawns all over North America and Europe. Have you seen me on your lawn? You can chew my leaves and then put them on a wound or sting to heal it. Can you find me?

A friendly adult can help you make a skin salve from plantain and other herbs. It can help heal minor burns, scrapes, dry flaky eczema, and a baby's diaper rash.

To make the salve, you will need:

> **4 or more cups of plantain, alone or with other herbs**
> **Enough good quality olive oil to cover the herbs**
> **Natural beeswax from an apiary or health food store**

1. Shred the herbs into small pieces with your hands. Place them in a large, nonaluminum pot.
2. Measuring 1 cup of oil at a time, add just enough olive oil to cover the herbs. (You will need to know later how many cups of oil you used, so write it down.)
3. In a separate pot, bring the beeswax to a simmer.
4. When both the herbs and the beeswax are simmering, for every 1 cup of olive oil that you put into the herbs earlier, now add 3 tablespoons of hot beeswax to the pot of herbs. Remove the beeswax from the heat.
5. Lower the heat under the herbs and let the whole mixture simmer, covered, for 20 minutes (do not let it boil!). Cool to room temperature and then strain into very clean glass jars. Wait until the jars are cool and then seal with lids. Store in a cool dark place.

Hint: you can also add other combinations to this salve. Try the green hulls of walnuts, fresh pine needles, poplar buds, elderberry leaves, comfrey, lavender, St. John's wort, calendula, or elecampane roots. When you do, be sure to add enough oil so that everything is well covered.

POKEWEED ☹
(Phytolacca americana)

I am pokeweed. You should *not* eat me because I am poisonous! I have bright, magenta-colored stalks and, in the fall, I have magenta berries. My root is fleshy and thick. I can grow up to 12 feet tall. Have you seen me? I am also called "ink berry" because you can write with my juicy berries.

Here's a fun thing to do with ripe pokeweed berries. Get a natural feather, such as a goose quill or a large seagull feather. Have a friendly adult help you make a quill pen by cutting the end of the quill so that it comes to a point (quill feather pens can also be purchased from many art stores). Put a handful of poke berries in a small bowl, and stick the quill into the berries several times to get enough "ink" on the pen. Then you can write or draw with it. Poke the pen back into the berries when it runs out of ink. (Clean up carefully because the seeds inside the berries are poisonous if ingested. The juice and flesh of the berries are not, but the juice does stain. Children should not eat any part of pokeweed.)

STINGING NETTLE
(Urtica dioica; U. urens)

I am the nettle. My stem is square and grows from 2 to 7 feet tall. My leaves are pointy with serrated edges and they sit opposite one another along my stem. I have small green flowers that appear from high summer to early fall. Be careful with me, I sting! But I am a very useful, edible plant. I am tastiest when I am no more than 6 inches tall. You must wear gloves when you pick me. Rinse my leaves carefully in cold running water and my sting will disappear. Chop my leaves and simmer them in soups to add minerals and iron. Add my dried leaf to other teas in the winter to keep your body warm and improve digestion. Can you find me?

You can make a wash to help soothe for minor burns and itchy skin problems. Steep 2 tablespoons of chopped nettle leaf in 1 cup of water for 10 minutes. Use when cool.

Young nettle greens are delicious when steamed, sautéed, or lightly boiled and served with butter. Nettles contain vitamin C, iron, and protein. They will even nourish your garden if you add them to your compost pile.

WILD STRAWBERRY
(*Fragaria vesca*)

I am the wild strawberry. I look just like those you buy in the store but am much smaller. I grow in shady areas near forests. You can make a vitamin-rich tea from my leaves. You can also eat my fruits and make them into jam.

To make strawberry tea, steep 2 teaspoons of strawberry leaf and/or root in freshly boiled water for 20 minutes. You can also use this tea as a wash for dry skin.

For a tasty strawberry treat, try making *Strawberry Honey*. To make it you will need:

16 ounces of light clover honey
½ cup fresh strawberries

1. Stir honey into a small saucepan over medium heat until it is thoroughly warmed. Do not boil.
2. Gently add the berries and stir lightly to cover with honey.
3. Pour into a clean jar (rinse the jar first with hot water to avoid thermal shock and possible breakage).
4. Close the jar and let stand for three days at room temperature, and then refrigerate.
5. Serve on waffles, breads, and pancakes.

TRILLIUM
(Trillium pendulum)

I am trillium. *Tri* comes from the Latin word meaning three. I have three leaves, three petals, and three sepals. One of my other names is "wake robin" because people believe that I wake up the robins in the spring and inspire them to sing. Native American women used me to ease the pain of childbirth, and I am sometimes called "birth root" or "beth root." My flowers can be white, yellow, or reddish. You will find me in the shady, damp woods. My seeds are carried to new places by friendly ants. The ants like the rich fat on the outside of my seeds and carry them back to their homes for dinner. The ants eat the fat but leave my seeds to grow into new plants. Can you find me?

I am a plant at risk of disappearing, so please do not pick me in the wild. I can live a very long time if people do not disturb me—one trillium plant is known to have lived for 72 years!

VIOLET
(*Viola spp.*)

I am the violet. I grow in wild shady areas such as thickets, around hedges, and along the edges of woods. My flowers can be purple or white. You can eat my leaves like spinach—they are very high in iron. Use my leaves, flowers, and roots in tea, or dry them for later use. My tea can help when you have a cough and it can help you sleep.

A fun thing to do with violet flowers is to make *Candied Violets* to put on cakes, cupcakes, and other desserts. To do this you will need:

Whole violet flowers
1 bowl of water for rinsing
1 cup water
1 ounce gum arabic
Tweezers
1 tablespoon corn syrup
1 cup finely granulated sugar plus ¹/₂ cup extra for sprinkling

1. Gently dip the flowers in the bowl of water to clean them. Dry them carefully on a paper towel, trying not to bruise the petals!
2. Dissolve the gum arabic into ¹/₂ cup of fresh water in a double boiler. Let the mix stand until cool. (You can put it in the refrigerator to speed up the process).
3. When cool, use tweezers to dip each violet into the gum arabic solution. Be sure to cover every surface (tweezers will help here).
4. Mix the corn syrup and 1 cup sugar in a stainless steel or enamel sauce pan with the remaining ¹/₂ cup of fresh water and bring to a boil. Cook until the syrup forms a ball when a spoonful is dropped in cold water. When the syrup is cool, you can dip the flowers into it. Lay the flowers on a paper towel and sprinkle with granulated sugar, then place them on waxed paper to dry.
5. Use the candied violets right away or store the flowers on layers of waxed paper in an airtight container in the refrigerator. If you prepare your flowers in this way they will keep for months.

YARROW
(Achillea millefolium)

I am yarrow. I have a round, smooth stem that can be slightly hairy. My white flowers grow in clusters at the tip of my stem and bloom from early summer to late fall. In the early spring you can find my feathery leaves in your lawn and in fields. At this time I am very good to put in salads as a spring green. (Add me to a salad of young dandelion greens!) Late in the year my leaves are good for stomach problems such as cramps, gas, and stomach flu. In olden times the pioneers called me "medicine plant" because I helped people so much.

Peppermint leaves, elderflowers, and yarrow were once a classic combination for treating flu and fever. To make a tea of yarrow, steep 1 tablespoon of dried leaves in 1 cup of freshly boiled water for about 30 minutes. Take 1 cup a day.

For external use, yarrow makes a healing wash for sores, minor wounds, and chapped hands. To make a wash, simmer 2 tablespoons of yarrow leaves in 1 cup of water for 20 minutes and let the liquid cool. Soak a soft old cloth in the liquid and apply it to the affected area.

Summer

First, April, she with mellow showers
Opens the way for early flowers;
Then after her comes smiling May,
In a more rich and sweet array;
Next enters June, and brings us more
Gems than those two, that went before:
Then, lastly, July comes, and she
More wealth brings in than all those three

**Robert Herrick,
"July: The Succession of
the Four Sweet Months"**

Buttercup nodded and said good-bye,
   Clover and daisy went off together,
But the fragrant water lilies lie
   Yet moored in the golden August weather.
The swallows chatter about their first flight,
   The cricket chirps like a rare good fellow,
The asters twinkle in clusters bright,
   While the corn grows ripe and the apples mellow.

**Celia Thaxter,
"August"**

BASIL
(Ocimum basilicum)

I am basil. My bushy stems reach 1 to 2 feet tall. My leaves have toothed edges and are deep green with a purplish tinge. My flowers can be white or red and appear from summer to early fall. Can you find me? You will often see me in the vegetable garden, but I am easy to grow in a pot on your windowsill. People like to put me in soups, sauces, spaghetti, and salads. I am very aromatic (I smell good!). You can use my leaves fresh or dried to make a tea for headaches, upset stomachs, sore throats, and coughs.

To make basil tea, steep 1 teaspoon of dried leaves or 2 teaspoons of fresh leaves in $1/2$ cup freshly boiled water for 20 minutes. Sweeten with honey for a cough. Take about 1 cup throughout the day in little sips.

Basil is a delicious kitchen herb. You can add chopped, fresh or dried, crumbled leaves to many dishes—fish, tomato sauce, pizza, or scrambled eggs.

BEE BALM
(Monarda spp.)

I am bee balm. My spiky pink, red, or purple flowers appear from summer to early fall. I am a relative of mint, so my stems are square. My opposite, serrated leaves are 3 to 6 inches long. I grow wild in moist clearings, and I am also an old-fashioned garden flower. I am very magical. When you plant me in your garden, I will attract butterflies and hummingbirds.

Related to peppermint, bee balm makes a nice tea to help soothe your stomach or bring down a fever. Steep 2 teaspoons fresh or 1 teaspoon dried flowers and leaves in freshly boiled water for 10 minutes. Bee balm tea adds a nice flavor to other teas too. You can also add bee balm leaves to salves for burns (see Plantain, page 61).

> To create a magical power spot in your garden, plant bee balm in a 3-foot wide circle and grow a carpet of thyme in the center. Sit in the middle and meditate, smelling the flowers and thyme as you inhale.

BLUEBERRY
(Vaccinium spp.)

I am the blueberry. I have alternate, oval-shaped leaves that are slightly toothed and shiny. My flowers are pink or red and white and appear in early summer. I grow in sandy areas in forests and fields. Have you ever eaten blueberry pancakes or blueberry pie? My berries ripen in late summer. They can be blue or blackish. A tea of my leaf can help fight diarrhea, coughs, and upset stomachs. A tea of my berries will help with fevers.

To make blueberry leaf tea, gather the leaves when the berries are still green. To make a tea from the leaves, steep 2 teaspoons of fresh, washed leaves in 1 cup of freshly boiled water for 20 minutes. Blueberry leaf tea should be used for only a few days.

To make tea from blueberries, simmer 1 teaspoon of dried blueberries in 1 cup of freshly boiled water for 20 minutes and chill. Drink up to 2 cups a day.

You can eat fresh blueberries to help cure mouth sores (good for sores from braces), clear lung congestion, and lessen intestinal gas—or just because they taste so good! If you have a mouth sore, hold the chewed berries in your mouth for a few seconds before swallowing. This will help the juices reach the irritated area.

CALENDULA
(*Calendula officinalis*)

I am calendula. Some of you call me "pot marigold." You will find me in the garden. From summer to fall, I have bright orange or yellow flowers that look like the sun. You can use my flowers and leaves in a tea for stomach problems, diarrhea, and fever, and boils. My flowers can be added to salves (see Plantain, page 61) to help heal sores, bruises, minor burns, and sprains. A tea or juice made from my flowers makes a good wash to help speed the healing of cuts and wounds.

To make a tea, steep 1 tablespoon of my fresh or dried flowers in $\frac{1}{2}$ cup of freshly boiled water for 20 minutes. Take 1 tablespoon every hour. Gargling with cold calendula tea after you have a tooth extracted can help stop the minor bleeding. (For heavy or serious bleeding, contact your dentist or orthodontist.)

You can also put my flowers and leaves in the juicer or blender (if you use a blender, you'll need to remove the pulp with a strainer). Take 1 teaspoon, freshly pressed, as an alternative to the tea.

Pick my flowers in the summer when they are newly opened and freeze them for use over the winter. Wash them, gently pat dry, and seal in a zip-top bag or plastic container with tight-fitting lid.

WILD CARROT
(Daucus carota)

I am the wild carrot. My white flowers look like lace. It was said that they looked like Queen Anne's lace headdress. That is why some people call me "Queen Anne's lace." Look for a tiny purple flower in the center of my blossoms. You must be careful not to confuse me with yarrow. Yarrow has larger flowers in smaller clusters and its leaves are not as lacy. You must also be very careful to not confuse me with poison hemlock. Hemlock has purplish stripes on its stalks and they are hairless. My stalks are green with small hairs on them. If you crush my leaves between your fingers they will smell like carrot. Have you seen me?

You can use small amounts of wild carrot root to flavor soups and stews, but it is very tough to chew and too much will turn your skin yellow. My seeds can be simmered (1 teaspoon per 1 cup of water) to make a remedy for upset stomach, gas, and coughs.

In the fall, you can collect the dried stems of Queen Anne's lace with their "bird's nests" of dried flowers on top. They look pretty in fall flower arrangements, plain or spray painted silver or gold.

> Gather a bouquet of Queen Anne's lace flowers and place them in a water-filled vase. Add a few drops of food coloring to the water, and watch the flowers change colors before your eyes!

CATNIP
(*Nepeta cataria*)

I am catnip. I grow from 1 to 3 feet tall in moist, shady areas. I am very soothing to your stomach and nerves, and I will help you get a good night's sleep. You can also use my dried leaves and flowering tops to treat bronchitis and diarrhea.

For catnip tea, steep 1 teaspoon of my leaves in a cup of freshly boiled water for 20 minutes. Take ¼ cup at a time, over several hours, up to 1 cup a day for a child; 2 cups for an adult.

Do you have a cat? Here's a fun activity: Offer your feline friend some catnip disguised as a mouse. Take a scrap of old fabric and cut out two matching teardrops about 4½ inches long and 3 inches at the widest part. Sew the two pieces together around the edge to make a little cloth bag shaped like a rain drop. Before you sew the two sides together completely, stuff the little bag with a few pinches of dried catnip. Finish closing the seams, tie a knot, and cut off the extra thread. Then sew a length of yarn to the fat, rounded end, and toss it to your cat who will go crazy!

> An old tradition suggests that you must carry catnip somewhere in your clothing if you want to communicate better with animals.

CHAMOMILE
(Chamaemelum nobile; Matricaria recutita)

I am chamomile. My leaves are feathery and light green. My flowers have white petals and little swollen yellow bellies that remind you of what I am good for—your stomach! Beside helping your tummy, I also help lower fevers, can help you sleep, and am a classic tea for teething babies.

> In Italy, farmers simmer honey, fresh mint leaves, chamomile flowers, and lemon rind together to make a tea that lulls its drinker to sleep.

To make a calming chamomile tea, steep 2 teaspoons of fresh or dried chamomile flowers in 1 cup of freshly boiled water for 20 minutes. Take a few sips every half hour until it is gone. (Babies can take 1 teaspoon every hour for 4 to 6 hours).

To make a relaxing bath (this is great for teething babies or unsettled youngsters), steep 1 pound of chamomile flowers in 5 quarts of freshly boiled water. Allow to cool, strain through a sieve or colander, and add to the tub.

Chamomile tea also makes a soothing wash for sores and minor wounds. Use a cotton ball to swab it on, or make a fomentation by soaking a clean cotton cloth in the tea, wringing it out, and wrapping it around the affected area.

CINQUEFOIL
(*Potentilla canadensis*)

I am cinquefoil. In French, *cinque* (pronounced "sank") means five. My leaves are divided into 5 sharply toothed leaflets. Can you count my leaves? I am also called "five-finger." My yellow flowers bloom from early spring to late summer. I grow in the grass. Can you find me?

To make a tea that helps stop diarrhea, makes sore throats feel better, and helps lower fevers, you will need 1 tablespoon of the chopped roots (they must be fresh or recently dried). Simmer the chopped roots in 1 cup of freshly boiled water for 20 minutes. Strain and take ¼ cup, 2 or 3 times a day.

Cinquefoil is a magical plant because it is shaped like a little hand. Its spirit will help you with all your projects. You can make a good-luck charm by pressing a cinquefoil leaf in a phonebook for a week. Mount it on a square of sturdy paper and cover with clear self-adhesive shelf paper.

An old legend says that cinquefoil also protects the home. To do this you must take an egg, carefully prick holes in both ends with a needle, and blow out the yolk (make a larger hole at one end). Fill the empty eggshell with a dried sprig of cinquefoil, tape the holes shut, and hide the egg somewhere in your house.

CLUB MOSS ☹
(Lycopodium obscurum; L. clavatum)

I am the club moss and you can find me on the forest floor. One variety of club moss, *L. clavatum*, sometimes called ground pine, is an evergreen with long, soft, fuzzy green runners that grows along the forest floor. Another variety, *L. obscurum*, is shiny with thin, smooth stems. Millions of years ago in the Devonian period, when only mosses and ferns covered the earth, I grew to a height of 33 feet! I am one of the oldest living things on earth. Can you find me?

During the Devonian age, many new plants and animals appeared. There were ferns and horsetails, and the first trees and forests grew. Animals called tetrapods walked on the land and swam in the water. Tetrapods were amphibians that looked like salamanders with big heads. Early relatives of spiders and fish also lived then.

You can travel back in time with an art activity and imagine what kinds of plants and animals lived so many millions of years ago. Here's how to make a Devonian collage. Press some club moss stems and ferns in an old phone book and pile a heavy book or two on top. When the plants are very flat and dry a week or two later, glue them onto a sheet of heavy paper to create a miniature forest scene of prehistoric times. On a separate sheet of paper paint or draw some Devonian creatures. Cut them out and glue them to your "forest."

COLTSFOOT
(Tussilago farfara)

I am coltsfoot. I am a strange plant because my round yellow flowers appear very early in the spring *before* my leaves! Later they turn white, almost like the puffballs of dandelions. My flowers look like little dandelions but my stem is grayish white and I have no dandelion greens. My leaves look like the footprint of a tiny horse. You will find me in moist areas such as swampy woods and near streams. Can you find me?

Coltsfoot makes a good external wash for alleviating discomfort from bug bites, minor burns, and sores. To make an external wash, steep 2 tablespoons of the fresh or dried flowers or leaves of the coltsfoot in 1 cup of freshly boiled water for 30 minutes and strain. Dip a washcloth or cottonball in the liquid and apply to the affected part.

> In medieval times coltsfoot was called "filium ante pater"—Latin for "the son before the father"—because the flowers bloom before the plant has leaves!

COMFREY
(*Symphytum officinale*)

I am comfrey. I have large hairy leaves and hairy stems. My flowers are white or purple and look like little bells. They bloom all summer long. I am usually found in people's gardens and sometimes grow wild in moist meadows. I am also called "knitbone" and "bruisewort" because I heal bones and bruises.

You can make what's called a *poultice*—a healing material placed on a cloth—to help heal sore parts of your body. Chop some comfrey leaves and place them in a blender with enough water to blend. Put the ground-up leaves in a bowl. Then add either slippery elm powder (a powdered tree bark available from herbalists) or buckwheat flour until you get a "pie dough" consistency. Spread this mixture on a clean cotton cloth and wrap it—gooey-side down—around a sprained, sore, or bruised part of your body. Leave this poultice on for 1 hour and then discard. Repeat daily as needed. You can use this poultice for minor burns and allergic swellings too. To use dried comfrey leaves for winter use, place in a bowl and pour hot water over them to make them soft, then proceed as directed in the recipe for a poultice. (Recent research indicates that comfrey should not be taken internally. The leaves are safe for external use.)

Hint: After you secure the whole poultice, it will be less messy if you then cover it all with plastic wrap and seal it with tape. This way the plant material won't fall out while you wait for the hour to pass.

DAISY
(Chrysanthemum leucanthemum)

I am the white "oxeye" daisy. My flower has a yellow disc in the middle surrounded by 20 to 30 white rays, or petals. I grow from 1 to 3 feet tall and have opposite, toothed leaves. You have probably seen me growing wild in fields. When they are very young my leaves and flowers can be added to salads. Make a tea of my leaves and flowers to help lower fevers and lessen coughs. To make oxeye daisy tea, use 2 teaspoons of my chopped, fresh or dried flowers and leaves for each cup of freshly boiled water. Steep for 20 minutes and strain. Add lemon and honey as desired. Drink 1 cup in $1/4$–cup doses throughout the day.

   Hint: For a very deep cough, try adding a tiny pinch of cayenne pepper or water from freshly boiled ginger root to the daisy tea. Adjust the amounts to your taste. Cayenne and ginger will make you sweat, so stay well covered.

> Have you ever made a daisy chain? If you find a field with many daisies, you can braid the stems together to form a garland. Secure the ends with thread. Wear it on your head and dance with the fairies!

DAYLILY
(Hemerocallis fulva)

I am the daylily. My large orange or yellow flowers open for only one day. That's how I got my name. I bloom all summer long. In China I am grown as a vegetable and sold in grocery stores! The Chinese call me "Little Golden Spears." You will find me in the flower garden where I am a hardy perennial (I come back every year). Have you seen me?

Add the spring leaves of daylilies to salads. The new buds of daylily flowers are delicious steamed or sauteed in olive oil. Opened flowers can be dipped in batter to make fritters or chopped and melted into soups as a thickener. You can eat the roots of the daylily all year round—raw in salads or boiled like a potato.

To make *Batter Fried Daylilies* you will need:

2 quarts fresh open daylily flowers
Oil for frying (olive oil is best)
1 cup flour
1 teaspoon salt
2 tablespoons melted butter
2 eggs, beaten
1 cup milk

1. Sift the salt and flour together. Mix in the butter and eggs. Beat in the milk a little bit at a time.
2. Add the oil to a large frying pan and heat on medium-high until the oil begins to sizzle.
3. Dip each flower into the batter and drop one at a time into the hot oil. Fry until golden brown. Place on paper towels briefly to absorb extra oil. Serve warm.

DILL
(Anethum graveolens)

I am dill. My leaves are feathery and blue-green. My flowers grow in umbrels—little inside out umbrellas—with tiny yellow flowers that bloom from summer to early fall. You can find me growing wild but I am usually found in people's vegetable gardens. A tea of my seeds helps relieve gas pains and can also help you sleep. You can chew my seeds as a natural breath sweetener.

To make a tea, steep 2 teaspoons of my seeds in 1 cup of freshly boiled water for 20 minutes. You can take up to 2 cups a day.

Chopped or minced dill is a wonderful herb to add to salads, soups, or steamed fish. Of course, it is also used to make pickles! To make dill pickles you will need the help of a grown-up and:

15 3–4-inch-long cucumbers
2 tablespoons apple cider vinegar
4 cloves garlic, peeled
1 teaspoon pickling spice
½ teaspoon mustard seed or
   celery seed

4 bay leaves
2 cups fresh dill, loosely packed
2 fresh grape leaves, optional
1 quart water
½ cup sea salt

You will also need 2 or 3 glass canning jars big enough to hold the cucumbers without being too big.

1. Sterilize the jars by placing them in a big pot and covering them with water. Bring to a boil and boil for 20 minutes. Pour off the water and use tongs to lift the jars onto a towel.
2. Clean the cucumbers and place them upright in two glass jars. Put half of the vinegar, garlic, pickling spice, mustard or celery seeds, bay leaves, and dill into each jar.
3. Bring the salt and water to a boil and pour over the cucumbers until there is ½ inch of space left at the top of each jar. Seal immediately and let stand in the refrigerator for 1 week. Eat within the next 3 weeks.

ECHINACEA
(*Echinacea angustifolia; E. purpurea*)

I am *Echinacea*. My stems are tall and bristly and my lovely pink flowers bloom from summer to fall. I am also called "purple coneflower" or sometimes "prairie coneflower" because I am a native of the tall grass prairies where the buffalo used to roam. Even though I love wide open spaces, I will do very well in your flower garden.

You can identify my different species if you look carefully at my flowers. *E. purpurea* has oval leaves with a little notch at the ends. It is the most common echinacea. *E. angustifolia* has short, smooth flower petals. Use the leaves and flowers of *E. purpurea* and the roots of *E. angustifolia*.

Echinacea is one of the best herbs for nipping a cold in the bud. Chop about 2 teaspoons of my root if using *E. angustifolia*. Place it in a saucepan with 1 cup of water, bring to a boil, lower the heat, and simmer for 20 minutes.

To make a tea of *E. purpurea,* take 2 teaspoons of my leaves and flowers and steep them in 1 cup of freshly boiled water for 20 minutes. Drink a cup of this tea every 2 hours until you feel well. Dry some roots and leaves for use over the winter.

> An easy way to dry herbs is to get sweater racks from your local dime store. They stack neatly and you can dry many layers of things in a cool, shady corner of the house. Never dry herbs in the sun because it ruins their healing properties.

ELDERBERRY
(*Sambucus canadensis; S. nigra*)

I am elderberry. I am called the "Elder-Mother" because I help children stay healthy. I am very sacred because I help people to get well. In Celtic countries, such as Ireland and Scotland, it is considered very unlucky to chop down my wood. I grow from 5 to 12 feet tall in the central and eastern United States and even taller in Europe. My bark is yellow-gray, and my leaves are opposite and serrated. You will see my flat bunches of white flowers from late spring to mid-summer. Hurry to gather my ripe berries in early fall—before the birds eat them! Look for me in moist, swampy areas and next to streams. Can you find me?

My berries are wonderful baked into pies or pancakes and made into jellies. When dried they make a nice tea that helps you fight off illness. Use 2 tea-spoons of dried berries per cup of water. Bring to a boil in a saucepan, reduce heat, and simmer for 20 minutes.

Elderberry flowers can be made into a tea that will make you sweat and help lower a fever. You can also eat them raw in salads and mix them (without their stems) into pancake batter. Make elder flower tea by steeping 2 teaspoons fresh or dried flowers per cup of freshly boiled water for $1/2$ hour. Drink it hot—up to $1 1/2$ cups a day (in $1/4$ doses) for a child, 3 cups for an adult.

The young leaves and young shoots of the elderberry are good for making healing salves, but *do not* use the leaves after the tree has flowered. (See Plantain, page 61, for salve directions).

> The elderberry is a very magical tree. In olden times people would pray before it (and some still do today!) to bring good health to themselves and their children. It has been said that by sprinkling elder flowers, berries, or leaves on a person or place, one can make wishes come true.

GINGER
(*Zingiber officinale*)

I am domesticated ginger. You will find me in your grocery store. Did you know that if you leave a piece of ginger root in a hot, humid place during the summer, it will sprout green buds? Plant the root in a flowerpot and place it on a sunny windowsill, and you will have a beautiful houseplant.

Ginger root makes a classic tea for digestive upsets. As an alternative, you can chew some candied ginger root when you have an upset stomach. Ginger tea also helps to warm the body and loosen secretions when you have the flu. Take 1 teaspoon of the root (about an inch), slice it, and boil it for 20 minutes in 1 pint of water. Add honey and lemon to taste. (For a really bad cold, try adding a tiny pinch of red pepper.) A child can take $1/4$ cup twice a day; an adult can have $1/4$ cup 4 times a day.

You can make your own ginger cough drops at home. To make them, you will need:

2 cups chopped ginger root
1 quart water
4–5 cups brown sugar
$1/2$ cup confectioners' sugar for sprinkling

1. Scrub the ginger roots thoroughly and rinse well. Chop into 1-inch pieces.
2. In an enamel or stainless steel pot, boil the pieces in the water for about 10 minutes, then simmer, covered, for another 30 minutes. Strain through a strainer or cheesecloth. Discard the pulp.
3. Add $1\frac{1}{2}$ cups brown sugar for every cup of remaining liquid.
4. Return to the pot and simmer, stirring until mixture thickens.
5. Pour into a greased 9 x 9 pan and spread to a thickness of about 1 inch. When the mixture begins to cool, cut the cough drops into small sections. Dust your hands with confectioners' sugar and roll the sections into balls.
6. Store in a tightly covered jar or container when completely cool.

Hint: Choose a cool, dry day to make your cough drops. They will be too sticky to work with if the weather is hot and humid!

GOLDENROD
(*Solidago odora*)

I am goldenrod. An old legend says that if I suddenly appear near your door, good luck will soon follow. I am a perennial and grow 2 to 4 feet tall. My leaves are thin with little dots on them, and my golden flowers bloom from summer to fall. I am usually found in open fields, mostly in the eastern half of the United States and in Europe. Have you seen me?

The fresh or dried leaves and flowers of goldenrod can be used to make a sweet-tasting tea that is good for you. Warm goldenrod tea is good for a cold because it makes you sweat; cold tea helps relieve gas. You can also soak a washcloth in the cool tea and apply it to your forehead if you have a headache. To make goldenrod tea, steep 2 teaspoons of leaves, flowers, or both, in 1 cup of freshly boiled water for 10 minutes. A child can have up to 1 cup per day (in $1/4$ cup doses); an adult can have up to 2 cups per day.

You can add goldenrod to a salve to help heal bee stings (see Plantain, page 61, for salve directions).

Caution: Anyone sensitive to ragweed pollen should avoid goldenrod.

> Hang small bunches of fresh, blooming goldenrod upside down in an attic or closet until they are dry. (Do not bundle them too tightly or air will not reach all the stems.) Once dry, they can be arranged in a vase. They will keep their golden color and remind you of the warmth of summer all winter long.

JERUSALEM ARTICHOKE
(Helianthus tuberosus)

I am the Jerusalem artichoke. I look like a small, wild sunflower. My leaves are large, oval, and rough on top. I have huge roots, or tubers, that look like potatoes. I grow as high as 10 feet tall in fields and disturbed areas. Have you seen me?

The roots of the Jerusalem artichoke can be eaten raw or cooked. You can pickle them in wine vinegar after boiling them for a short time. They are especially good for diabetics because unlike the potato they have very little starch when they are very fresh. Slice raw Jerusalem artichokes for a delicious addition to salads. Boil them and flavor with butter, lemon juice, parsley, or chives for another great taste.

> If you can find Jerusalem artichokes in the summer when they are blooming, mark the spot. Then you will be able to dig the roots all fall and winter.

LAVENDER
(Lavandula angustifolia)

I am lavender. I grow from 1 to 2 feet high. My opposite leaves are grayish green, long and thin and downy. My tiny flowers are—guess what?—lavender and appear up and down my stem from summer to early fall. My flowers and leaves smell wonderful. People sew me into little bags and tuck me into closets and drawers to scent their clothing and to repel moths. (For very effective moth repellant, dry me and mix me with some cedar chips purchased from your local pet store.) It happens that I am also an *esculent* which means I am an edible plant. Here are some fun things to do with my flowers:

To make *Lavender Sugar:* For each ¾ cup of granulated sugar, add 1 teaspoon dried lavender flowers. Grind with a mortar and pestle or use a food processor.

For your own homemade *Lavender Ice Cream* you will need:

> 1½ cups milk
> 2½ cups light cream
> 1 teaspoon vanilla extract
> 8 egg yolks
> ¾ cup lavender sugar (see above)
> ¼ teaspoon salt

1. Combine the milk, cream, and vanilla and in the top portion of a double boiler and bring to a simmer.
2. In a separate bowl, whisk together the egg yolks, lavender sugar, and salt. Add some of the milk mixture, and then pour all of the egg yolk mixture into the double boiler. Heat, stirring constantly, until the mixture thickens enough to coat a metal spoon.
3. Fill the sink with cold water and ice cubes. Set the double boiler into the ice water—being sure the water doesn't rise over the edge—until cool. Place the mixture into the refrigerator until it is very cold.
4. When chilled, pour into a hand-cranked or electric ice cream maker and follow instructions provided with the machine.

LEMON BALM
(Melissa officinalis)

I am lemon balm. I am also called "Melissa." I grow up to 3 feet tall and have opposite oval leaves that are hairy and slightly serrated. My flowers grow in clusters of pale yellow, rose, or light blue and appear at the height of summer. You can tell that I am related to mint because my stems are square. I am often found in the garden and sometimes in wild places like fields and roadsides. My leaves and flowers smell lemony when you rub them between your hands! You can dry my leaves and flowers and put them in sachets and herb pillows. Bees like me so much that bee keepers rub my fresh herb on their new hives to attract other bees and to help the bees that live there find their way home. Have you seen me?

Lemon balm makes a relaxing tea that helps headaches, fevers, toothaches, coughs, upset stomachs and cramps. To make lemon balm tea, steep 2 teaspoons of chopped, fresh leaves and flowers in 1 cup of freshly boiled water for 20 minutes. You can also make a large batch and add it to your bath before bedtime to help you sleep.

Lemon balm is a great herb for the kitchen too. You can add the whole or chopped leaves to salads, poultry stuffing, fish, and lamb. Whole leaves can be used to decorate cakes and floated in an iced tea or punch.

To repel bugs, rub lemon balm leaves on your skin. Bees love the smell, but other bugs hate it (don't try this if there are a lot of bees around!).

MARJORAM
(Wild—*Origanum vulgaris*; Domestic—*Marjorana hortensis*)

I am marjoram. I am native to north Africa, but now I grow in many other places too, including the United States and Europe. I am a perennial in southern areas but I am sometimes an annual in the north. I grow up to 1 foot tall. My tiny white or pink flowers grow in clusters of 3 to 5 at the top of my spiky stems from late summer to early fall. My leaves are fuzzy, opposite, and gray-green. You can recognize me by rubbing my leaves between your hands—I smell very aromatic!

According to magical tradition, I bring joy. The ancient Greeks wore wreaths of marjoram at weddings because it was sacred to Aphrodite, the goddess of love. They also used marjoram wreaths at funerals because they thought it helped people feel less sad. I also help with seasickness, indigestion, and upset stomachs. Place my dried leaves and flowers in a corner of your pillowcase to help you sleep. If you include some dried hops *(Humulus lupulus),* it will be even more effective.

To make marjoram tea, steep 2 teaspoons of my herb per cup of freshly boiled water for 20 minutes. Drink up to 2 cups a day to relieve minor stomach ailments. You can make a big batch of the tea and add it to your bath to help you sleep.

Marjoram is tasty in many kinds of foods. Add fresh or dried marjoram to stuffings, salads, meats, poultry, soups, sausage, potatoes, tomatoes, squash, and egg dishes. Try it on pizza!

MINT
(Mentha spp.)

I am mint. I grow prolifically in many different varieties, usually in a cool and shady spot. I grow wild near streams and am also planted in people's gardens. My leaves and square stems are usually dark green (chocolate mint has brown stems!). I have tiny purple flowers that bloom from summer to early fall. It's easy to identify me: rub a leaf between your hands and sniff. I smell minty. I am an herbal classic. As a tea, I am very good for your tummy aches, mild fevers, and the stomach bug. I can help you relax and fall asleep and ease your headache.

To make mint tea: steep 2 teaspoons of dried, crumbled or fresh, chopped-mint leaves in 1 cup of freshly boiled water. Let it steep for 20 minutes. When your skin itches or if you have a minor burn, put mint tea in your bath or make a fomentation to soothe the affected area. To do this, simply dip a clean cotton cloth into the cooled tea and wrap it around the affected part. Leave it on for about an hour. To keep it from dripping, you can cover the cloth with plastic wrap.

A delicious way to flavor honey is by adding fresh herbs. You can make honey flavored with mint, as well as rosemary, lavender, thyme, and organic lemon or orange peels.

To make *Mint Honey,* put about 16 ounces of honey in a pot and stir over a medium heat until warmed. Add 7 sprigs of clean, fresh mint and pour into a clean, heat-proof jar. Cool to room temperature, cover with a tight lid, and let stand for 7 days. Check the jar daily to make sure the honey is not becoming too strongly flavored. When the flavor is right, strain out the herbs (you can leave a leaf or two behind to make the honey look pretty).

> You can dry mint to use during the winter. Just cut some stems of mint after the morning dew has dried, tie them in loose bunches, and hang them upside down in a dry closet or attic. When they are dry, remove the leaves from the stems and store in a clean, covered mason jar.

NASTURIUM
(Tropaeolum majus)

I am nasturtium. I am a climbing garden flower that originally came from Peru. I can grow to be 5 to 10 feet long. My yellow, orange, or red flowers bloom from summer to fall. They taste peppery and delicious! I am as beautiful as I am spicy. Have you seen me?

Nasturtium blossoms are tasty and helpful. They are a natural disinfectant, and you can put their juice on a minor scratch or cut. Many people like to eat nasturtium flowers in salads. I am also delicious in sandwiches. Try making some open-faced cream cheese sandwiches decorated with nasturtium blossoms. To help relieve a chest cold, put nasturtium flowers and leaves in a juicer (or in the blender with a little water), strain, and drink the fresh juice in $1/2$ teaspoon doses.

> An old magical tradition says that having three red flowers planted in the garden will keep away unwanted visitors. Nasturtiums, red hollyhocks, roses, bee balm, poppies, and geraniums are some of the flowers you can use for this purpose.

PARSLEY
(Petroselinum sativum)

I am parsley. Cooks like to use me for flavoring and as a garnish. I am easy to grow in your garden and I will come up year after year. My leaves are feathery and shiny and very green. They look a lot like celery leaves. My white (or greenish white) flowers appear in the summer. If you pinch back my flowers, I will keep making greens for you (leave a few to go to seed and collect them for next year's garden). Take me out of the garden in September, put me in a flowerpot, and place me on a sunny windowsill—you will have fresh parsley all winter long! Have you seen me? I am the plant that the ancient Romans hid in their togas as a form of protection. The ancient Greeks made crowns of my leaves for the winners of the Isthmian games. They also placed wreaths of parsley on graves.

Try adding fresh, chopped parsley to salads, tuna fish, soups, and egg dishes. Parsley is a great source of vitamins A, B, and C as well as calcium, iron, and other trace minerals. Nibble a sprig of parsley to freshen your breath. Make a tea of the leaves or seeds to treat intestinal gas or coughs (but *do not* use parsley if you have an inflammatory kidney condition). Steep 1 teaspoon of chopped, fresh parsley leaves or simmer 2 teaspoons of parsley seeds in 1 cup of freshly boiled water for 20 minutes.

POPLAR

QUAKING ASPEN
(Populus tremuloides)

BALM-OF-GILEAD, (TACAMAHAC)
(Populus balsamifera)

BLACK POPLAR
(Populus nigra)

We are the poplar trees. Our toothed leaves tremble and shake in the wind. Have you seen us? All poplars have buds that make good medicine. Our buds can be simmered into salves (see page 61) to soothe cuts, swellings, scratches, and minor burns.

A poplar-bud tea is good for coughs, sore throats, and minor muscle aches and pains. Simmer 2 teaspoons of the sticky winter buds per cup of freshly boiled water for 20 minutes. You can also use the tea as a wash to treat cuts and scratches, swellings, and minor burns. (Avoid using poplar if you are allergic to its pollen.)

> An old tradition says that poplar leaves carry messages to the gods on their trembling leaves. Tell a poplar tree about your dreams.

PURSLANE
(Portulaca oleracea)

I am purslane. Many people think of me as a weed. A weed is a plant whose uses have yet to be appreciated! I am a dark green fleshy plant with red stems and I grow very low to the ground. My flowers are small and white. In olden times soldiers carried me as a charm to protect themselves in battle. People would dry my leaves and strew me around the house to bring happiness and prevent nightmares.

Purslane is rich in vitamins such as A and C and minerals such as calcium, iron, and phosphorus. Purslane can be eaten raw or cooked. Wash the herb carefully and soak it for 20 minutes in water to which you've added salt or vinegar. Chop the stems and leaves and add them to salad. You can also boil, steam, or sauté (with garlic!) them until soft and serve with butter. Add chopped purslane to soups and stews for extra iron. The ground seeds of purslane can be added to flour. The pickled stems and leaves of purslane can be saved for winter use as a vegetable.

Caution: Purslane is best avoided by those with sensitive stomachs.

RASPBERRY
(*Rubus strigosus; R. idaeus*)

I am the raspberry. You may have seen my prickly, rambling branches in the garden or in the wild. Have you tasted my delicious red berries? My leaves make a wonderful tea that helps diarrhea and nausea. Pregnant women and unsure boaters appreciate my tea because it helps with the nausea of morning sickness and seasickness.

Drink the fresh juice of raspberries to help bring down a fever and strengthen the heart. Eating raspberries will make your blood healthy and strong. Drink raspberry leaf tea to help with diarrhea or nausea.

To make raspberry tea, steep 2 tablespoons of leaves in 1 cup of freshly boiled water for 20 minutes. You can also use the tea externally as a wash for sores, rashes, itches, and minor cuts.

Raspberry Honey is a delicious way to preserve your summer harvest of raspberries. To make it you will need:

16 ounces clover honey
1/2 cup fresh raspberries

1. Place honey in a saucepan and stir over medium heat until warmed. Do not boil.
2. Gently add the berries.
3. Temper a clean jar first with hot water to avoid thermal shock and breakage. Pour out the water and pour the honey mixture into the jars.
4. Close the jar tightly and let sit for 3 days at room temperature.
5. Keep refrigerated. Serve on waffles, bread, and pancakes.

RED CLOVER
(Trifolium pratense)

I am wild clover. I have round, pinkish purple flowers and my leaves have three oval leaflets. I grow in meadows. Cows like to eat me and people do too! Bees love my pollen. You can use my fresh blossoms in salads and sandwiches—they will float on your soup!

Clover tea is a mild pick-me-up that improves digestion, soothes coughs, and promotes regular bowel movements. It is good to take after an illness or to revive your appetite.

To make a tea, steep 2 teaspoons of red clover's fresh or dried flowers in $^1/_2$ cup of freshly boiled water for 10 minutes. Drink up to $1^1/_2$ cups by the teaspoonful throughout the day. An external wash of clover tea helps stop the itch of bug bites. You can soak a cloth in the warm tea and wrap the affected part.

White clover (Trifolium repens) has similar properties to red clover but it is not quite as powerful as an herb. All clover attracts bees. Plant clover around your fruit trees to assist pollination.

ROSE
(Rosa spp.)

I am the rose. I am well known. I come in many colors, sometimes by the dozen. I have a thorny stem. When I am red I am the best kind of rose for eating and for herbal medicine. Put my petals in vinegar to make a compress for headaches. Eat them in salads or on ice cream and add them to jellies. Candy my petals and put them on cakes and cupcakes (see Violet, page 71).

In the fall, after the first frost, you can gather bright red rose hips. (Be sure to gather rose hips or petals from wild or organically cultivated roses that have not been sprayed.) They look like shiny little red apples and have more vitamin C than lemons. Carefully open them and remove the seeds and hairs. Dry them in a dry, dark, cool place for later use as tea. Rose hip tea with honey and lemon is one of the best remedies for a sore throat. To make rose hip tea, place 2 teaspoons of rose hips and 1½ pints of water in a pot over medium-high heat. Bring to a boil, reduce heat to low, and simmer for 10 minutes. Fill a mug or tea cup and add honey and lemon as desired.

To make a tea from rose petals, use 2 teaspoons of dried or fresh rose petals per cup of water and steep for 20 minutes. Drink a tea of rose petals for headaches and to help you relax. Gargle with rose petal tea to help heal mouth sores.

ROSEMARY
(*Rosmarinus officinalis*)

I am fragrant rosemary. My leaves are thin and spiky and leathery. My flowers are pale blue or white and appear from spring to summer. You can grow me on a sunny windowsill or in your yard. Most people know me as a kitchen herb but I also have medicinal uses. You can add my leaves to healing salves (see Plantain, page 61) or to a bath to soothe sore muscles. In ancient Greece, students wore wreaths of rosemary in their hair to improve their memory. You can try sniffing a sprig of rosemary to help you concentrate while you study.

Making *Rosemary Herb Jelly* is one fun way to use rosemary. To make it you will need:

1 cup chopped, fresh rosemary
2½ cups distilled water
¼ cup orange juice, cider vinegar, or lemon juice
4½ cups sugar
3 ounces liquid pectin

1. Place the water in a non-aluminum saucepan and bring to a boil. Remove from heat, add rosemary, and steep for 2 minutes.
2. Strain the liquid from the mix into a second pot and place over medium-high heat.
3. Add orange juice (or cider vinegar or lemon juice) and sugar and bring to a rolling boil, stirring constantly.
4. Add pectin and bring to a rolling boil again. Boil for one minute.
5. Remove from heat, skim off foam, and discard foam.
6. Ladle into tempered, sterilized jars, leaving about ½ inch of space at the top. Seal jars tightly. Let cool for 24 hours. May be stored, refrigerated, for up to 2 months.

To make other herb jellies, you can do the same with parsley, lavender, scented basil, rose geranium, fennel, lemon balm, or lemon verbena. Use orange or lemon juice with the sweeter herbs, vinegar with the spicy ones.

SAGE
(Salvia officinalis)

I am sage. My square stems are slightly hairy and woody at the bottom. I have opposite, downy leaves with very fine crinkles in them. My purple, blue, or white flowers grow in whorls and appear in the summer. You will probably find me in someone's garden. My leaves are very dry with almost no sap in them. That is why I am a good herb to take for "wet" colds—colds with a lot of mucus. I can help dry up your nose and chest and lower your fever.

To make sage tea, use 2 teaspoons of chopped, fresh sage leaves per cup of freshly boiled water and steep for 20 minutes. (Add lemon to make the tea even more effective against wet colds). Because it is naturally antiseptic, sage tea also makes a nice wash for scrapes and scratches. Sage is a strong herb and should only be taken for a short time (a few days at most).

To soothe a sore throat, you can make a sage gargle. Pour $1/2$ cup of hot apple cider vinegar and $1/2$ cup of freshly boiled water over 2 teaspoons of chopped, fresh sage leaves and steep for 30 minutes. Add honey if you like. Use warm or cool. This will help with mouth sores and bleeding gums too.

> Did you know that toads love sage? Plant some in the garden to attract them.

139

STAGHORN SUMAC
(Rhus typhina)

I am the staghorn sumac. My leaves are finely toothed. My branches look like the giant horns of a mule deer. I have greenish yellow flowers and then I grow fuzzy clusters of hairy red fruits that are ripe in summer. You will find me along the edges of fields and roads where I grow in thick stands. Have you seen me?

You can make "Indian lemonade" from the berries of the staghorn sumac. Just put the red clusters in a non-aluminum pot or bowl and cover with boiling water. Let the berries sit for about 15 minutes and then strain the pink tea into a mug or pitcher. Add honey to taste. This tea can help with diarrhea, fevers, mouth sores, and sore throats, and it also makes a fine wash for minor cuts or scrapes.

> Be careful not to confuse poison sumac and stagorn sumac! Poison sumac grows in or around swamps and has clusters of white berries and toothless leaves.

SUNFLOWER
(*Helianthus annuus*)

I am the mighty sunflower. I have BIG flowers that bloom from summer to fall—a round brown center with golden petals that remind you of the sun. I can grow up to 12 feet tall! My leaves are rough and my stems are hairy. You can find me in fields and prairies and in sunny gardens. I am a native plant of Mexico and of Peru where I was once considered sacred by the Aztecs and worshipped by the Incas. Priestesses would carry my flowers in the temples of the sun and wear crowns of them in their hair. I was honored so highly that sculptures of my flowers were made out of pure gold and placed in Aztec shrines. Have you seen me?

Sunflower seeds make a good snack—birds and hamsters love them too! You can sprinkle them (without their shells) on salads to add crunch. Sunflower seed butter, available from health food stores, can be spread on bread or bagels, alone or with jam.

One fun thing to do with sunflower seeds is to make a picture by gluing them on cardboard or wood. You can mix them with other seeds and grains (dried beans and peas are very colorful) for different colors and textures. This kind of picture is called a *mosaic*. You might choose to make a shining sun or flowers or something else that celebrates the season of summer and the harvest.

Find a square of cardboard, wood, poster board, or another sturdy surface and sketch your design with a pencil. Using nontoxic craft glue (just a dab for each seed), attach the seeds close together to form the desired shape. Let your mosaic dry overnight before moving it. These beautiful seeds will remind you of the life and sunshine stored in tiny packages over the long winter!

> You can take 10–15 drops of cold-pressed sunflower oil several times a day to help with a cough or a chest cold.

143

THYME
(Domestic— *Thymus vulgaris;* Wild— *Thymus serpyllum)*

I am thyme. My creeping stems are woody and grow from 6 to 10 inches long. My opposite leaves are tiny and smell spicy. I grow in people's gardens and also wild in the hills and forests. I have purple flowers that bloom from spring to fall.

Thyme is used in cooking and also makes a wonderful tea for sore throats, bronchitis, laryngitis, and any mucousy lung conditions. It also relieves diarrhea, upset stomachs, and headaches. Thyme tea can help you get to sleep.

To make thyme tea, use 2 teaspoons of fresh or dried herb per cup of freshly boiled water. Steep for 10 minutes. (Thyme tea is not for longterm use. Drink only about ¾ cup [child's dose] a day for just a few days.)

Thyme tea can be added to bath water. Thyme baths are very good for calming the nerves and for soothing bruises, swellings, sprains, and muscle aches and joint pains. For a bath you will want to make the tea much stronger. Use about 4 ounces of thyme steeped in enough boiling water to cover for 30 to 45 minutes. Strain and add to bath water.

> Remember that every garden has a bit of garden magic. Wherever thyme grows naturally you will find an energizing power spot on the earth. If you want to create a power spot in *your* garden, plant a circular blanket of thyme.

WILLOW ☹
(Salix spp.)

I am willow. Do you know anyone named Sally? If you do, she is someone named after me, the graceful willow tree. The name *Sally* is a variation on my Latin species name *Salix*. "Sally rods," or willow branches, are used in Ireland to thatch traditional farmhouses. There are many different willow species across the United States. We all love water. Some of us have drooping branches (like the weeping willow), and some of us have branches that stick straight up. Some of us are as big as trees and others are small shrubs. Our branches tend to be pliable, and people use them to make baskets.

You can often find another type of willow in the spring, *Salix nigra*. It is called the "pussy willow" because its buds are gray and furry like a little kitten. Look for willows near streams and in damp fields. Have you seen us?

The bark of willows is known to lower fevers and reduce pain. This is because it contains a chemical called "salicin," which converts into "salicylic acid" in your body. Commercial aspirin is really a synthetic form of willow bark. (Because willow bark contains an aspirin-like substance, *children should not take it internally*. Aspirin is associated with Reye's syndrome, a rare but potentially fatal disease that can follow a viral infection.) You can collect some bark from willow branches in the spring and simmer it to make an external wash for minor cuts, abrasions, and stinky feet. Use 1 to 3 teaspoons of my bark per cup of water and simmer for 20 minutes in a non-aluminum pot with a tight lid.

> Willows will only grow if there is water in the area. If you live in a damp area, you can easily propagate a willow tree. Just stick a freshly cut willow twig in the moist ground in the early spring and it will sprout.

WITCH HAZEL
(Hamamelis virginina)

I am the witch hazel. I am a very small tree with stringy, strange yellow flowers that appear in autumn when my leaves start to fall. My gray bark is smooth. You will usually find me in the wild woods, although some people grow me in their lawns for my autumn flowers. Dowsers have used my branches as divining rods since ancient times. (A *divining rod* is a forked branch that is believed to dip down when it is held over an area of land where water or minerals lie beneath the surface.) Dowsers would use the rods to find underground currents of water. That is how I got my name—because witches are good at dowsing and because they practice the ancient healing art of herbalism using *witch hazel* and other trees and flowers.

The leaves and bark of witch hazel can be gathered in the spring to make a tea for diarrhea and a mouthwash for sore throats and mouth sores, a tea for diarrhea, and an external wash for minor burns, bug bites, bruises, and itchy rashes.

To make witch hazel tea, simmer one teaspoon of my bark or leaf in 1 cup of water for 20 minutes in a covered pan. Take up to 1 cup a day in 1/4-cup doses. To soothe tired or inflamed eyes, you can strain this tea and dip a cloth in it to make an eye compress. (Remember to keep your eyes closed while the cloth covers them.) Adding the tea to your bath can give your body a good all-over soak.

EPILOGUE

And so we come to the end of another sacred Earth year, the leaves on the trees beginning to fade, the blazing light of summer starting to wane. We have brought home the harvest of woodlands, fields, and gardens. Soon we will be dreaming of the dark season of snow. Can another spring be far behind?

BIBLIOGRAPHY

Bennett, Philis "Savoring the Bee's Kiss." *Victoria Magazine* 4, no. 8 (August 1990): 88–99.

Clairborne, Craig. *The New York Times Cook Book.* New York: Harper and Row, 1961.

Crowhurst, Adrienne. *The Weed Cookbook.* New York: Lancer Books, 1972.

Cunningham, Scott. *Cunningham's Encyclopedia of Magical Herbs.* St. Paul, Minn.: Llewellyn Publications, 1986.

Foster, Steven, and James A. Duke. *A Field Guide to Medicinal Plants and Herbs: Eastern and Central North America.* Boston: Houghton Mifflin, 2000.

Grieve, M. *A Modern Herbal.* New York: Dover Publications, 1971.

Harris, Benjamin Charles. *Kitchen Medicines.* Worcester, Mass.: Natura Publications, 1961.

Hopman, Ellen. *A Druid's Herbal for the Sacred Earth Year.* Rochester, Vt.: Destiny Books, 1994 .

———. *Tree Medicine, Tree Magic.* Custer, Wash.: Phoenix Publishers, 1991.

Kowalchik, Claire, and William H. Hylton, eds. *Rodale's Illustrated Encyclopedia of Herbs.* Emmaus, Penn.: Rodale Press, 1987.

Lust, John. *The Herb Book.* New York: Bantam Books, 1982.

Pahlow, Mannfried. *Living Medicine.* Wellingborough, Northamptonshire, England: Thorsons Publishers, Ltd., 1982.

Peterson, Lee Allen. *A Field Guide to Edible Wild Plants.* Boston, Mass.: Houghton Mifflin Company, 1977.

Rodale Press. *Field Guide to Wild Herbs.* Emmaus, Penn.: Rodale Press, 1989.

Tierra, Michael. *Planetary Herbology.* Santa Fe, N.M.: Lotus Press, 1988.

Tolley, Emelie. "A Nuance of Lavender," *Victoria Magazine,* 5, no. 8 (August 1991): 30.

———. "From an Herb Lover's Garden", *Victoria Magazine,* 5, no. 9 (September 1991): 40.

RESOURCES

To receive more information and publications on medicinal herbs, please contact the following:

American Botanical Council
P. O. Box 144345
Austin, TX 78714-4345
www.herbalgram.org

The American Herbalists Guild
1931 Gaddis Road
Canton, GA 30115
www.healthy.net/herbalists

The American Herb Association
P.O. Box 1673
Nevada City, CA 95959
www.jps.net/ahaherb

Herb Research Foundation
1007 Pearl Street, Suite 200
Boulder, CO 80302
www.herbs.org